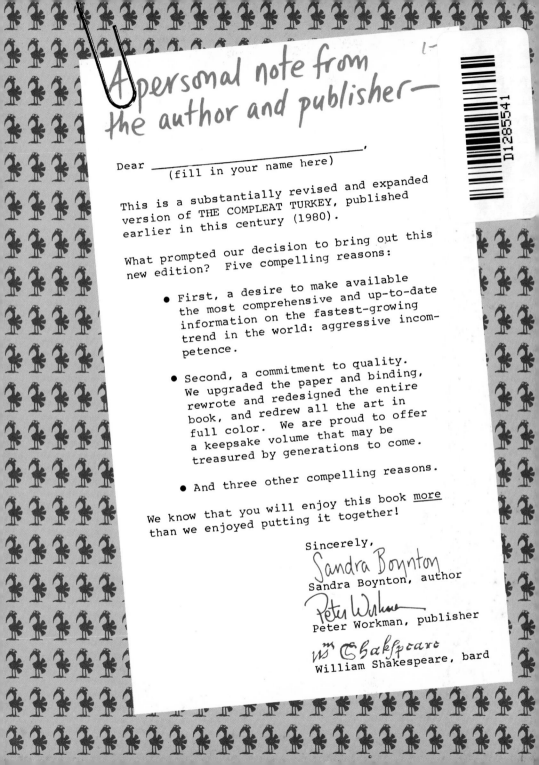

A personal note from
the author and publisher—

Dear _____,
　　　(fill in your name here)

This is a substantially revised and expanded
version of THE COMPLEAT TURKEY, published
earlier in this century (1980).

What prompted our decision to bring out this
new edition? Five compelling reasons:

- First, a desire to make available
  the most comprehensive and up-to-date
  information on the fastest-growing
  trend in the world: aggressive incom-
  petence.

- Second, a commitment to quality.
  We upgraded the paper and binding,
  rewrote and redesigned the entire
  book, and redrew all the art in
  full color. We are proud to offer
  a keepsake volume that may be
  treasured by generations to come.

- And three other compelling reasons.

We know that you will enjoy this book _more_
than we enjoyed putting it together!

Sincerely,

Sandra Boynton
Sandra Boynton, author

Peter Workman
Peter Workman, publisher

Wm Shakespeare
William Shakespeare, bard

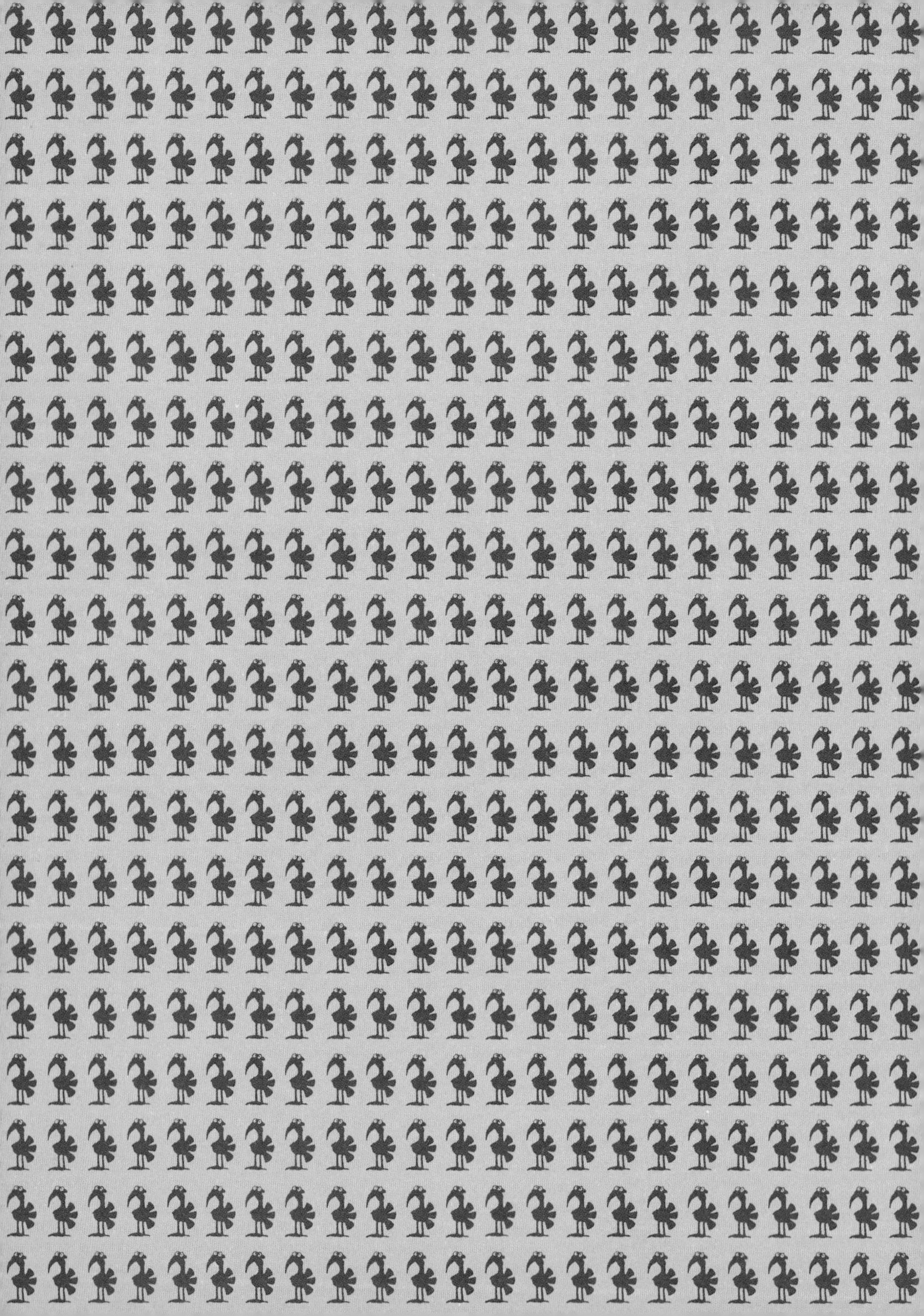

Boynton's

DON'T LET THE TURKEYS GET YOU DOWN

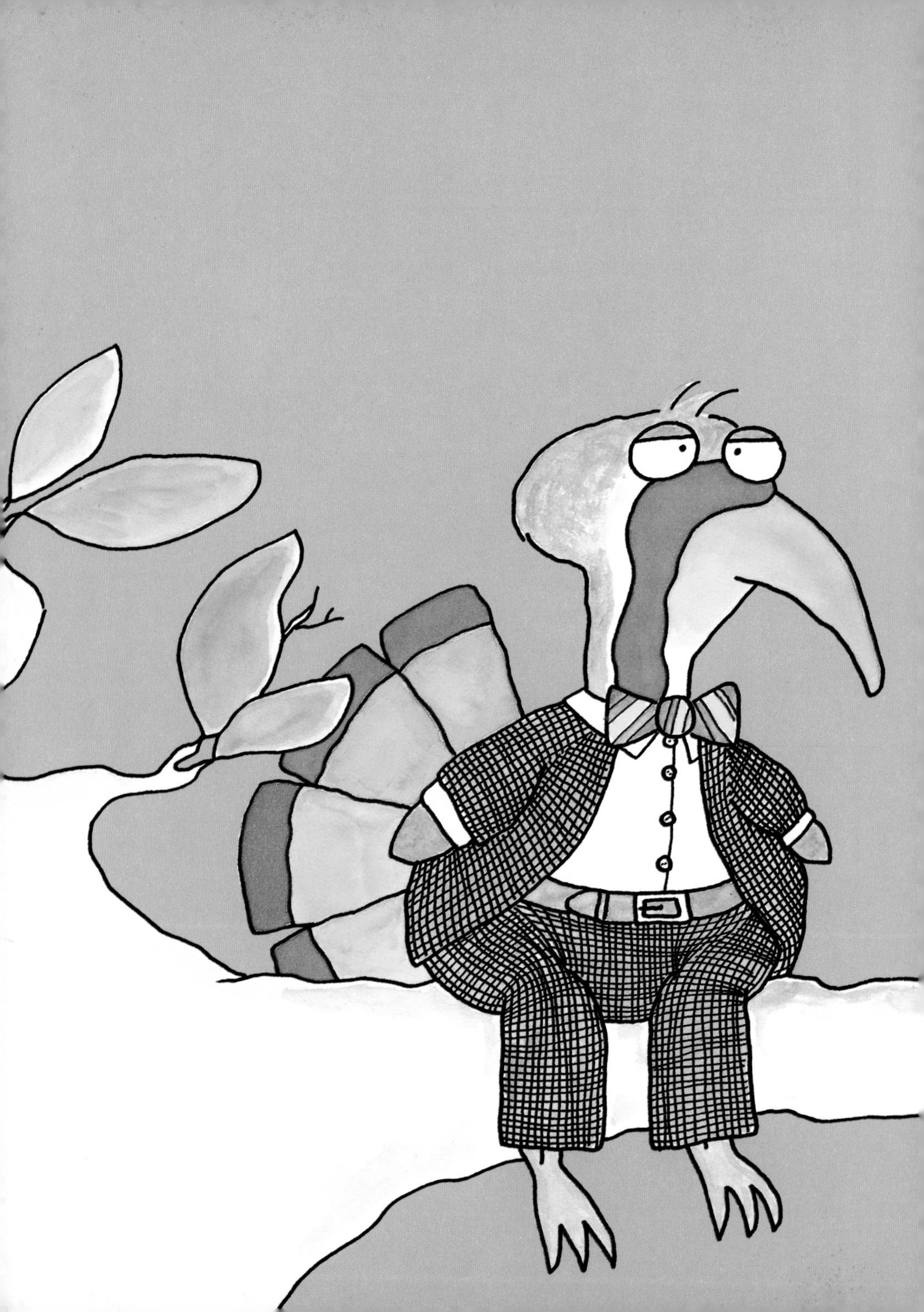

DON'T LET THE TURKEYS GET YOU DOWN

By Sandra Boynton, Ph.T.

WORKMAN PUBLISHING
NEW YORK

Turkey Lurkey to all points:
SKY IS FALLING.
Repeat:
SKY IS FALLING. Over.

Copyright © 1986 by Sandra Boynton

Library of Congress Cataloging-in-Publication Data

Boynton, Sandra.
Don't let the turkeys get you down.
Rev. ed. of: The compleat turkey. c1980.
Summary: Presents descriptions of the various
"turkeys" of contemporary life in all fields—repairmen,
restaurateurs, professionals—as well as comments on
"turkeys" in general.
1. Failure (Psychology)—Anecdotes, facetiae,
satire, etc. [1. Wit and humor] I. Boynton, Sandra.
Compleat turkey. II. Title.
PN6231.F28B68   1985   741.5'973   85-26308
ISBN 0-89480-013-2

Book design: Paul Hanson

Workman Publishing Company, Inc.
1 West 39 Street
New York, NY 10018

Manufactured in the United States of America

First printing April 1986

10 9 8 7 6 5 4 3 2 1

A small portion of the text in *Don't Let the Turkeys Get You Down*
originally appeared in *The Compleat Turkey,* copyright © 1980 by Sandra Boynton.

ANY SIMILARITY TO ACTUAL PERSONS, LIVING OR
IN LOS ANGELES, IS STRICTLY UNINTENTIONAL,
INCLUDING THE STUFF ON PAGE 54 THAT WILL
REMIND MANY PEOPLE OF SNIGBERT KNUDDSEN.

To Whom It May Concern

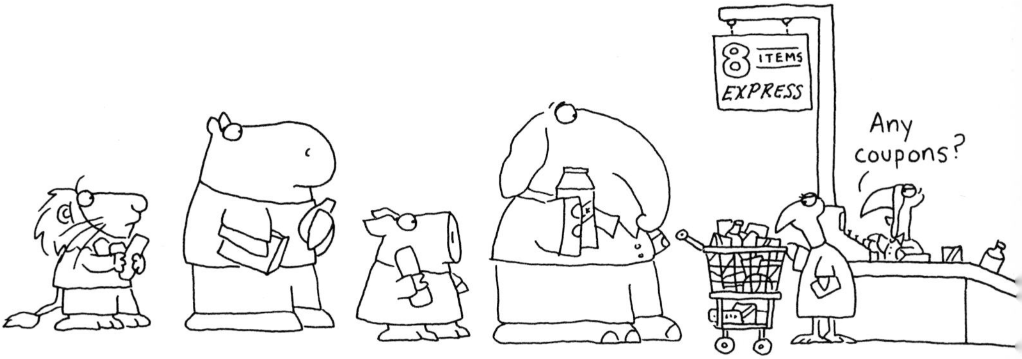
8 ITEMS
EXPRESS
Any coupons?

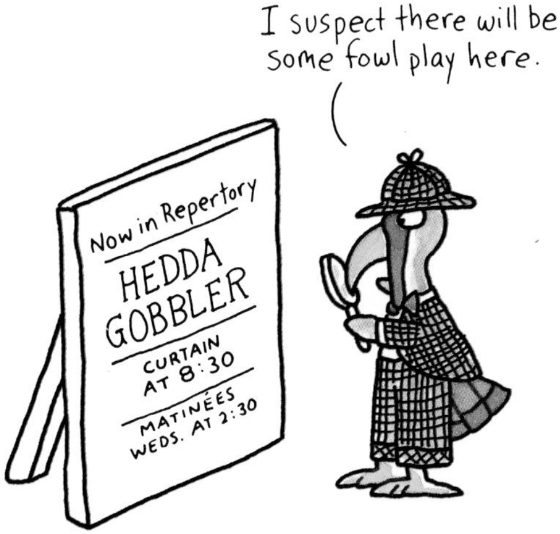
I suspect there will be some fowl play here.
Now in Repertory
HEDDA GOBBLER
CURTAIN AT 8:30
MATINÉES WEDS. AT 2:30

CONTENTS

PREFACE
THE MEANING AND DERIVATION OF "TURKEY"

The *Random House College Dictionary* (1979) defines "Turkey" as "a republic in W Asia and SE Europe." This isn't at all helpful, and may help explain why dictionary sales are down.

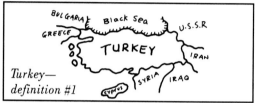

Turkey— definition #1

We find more pertinent information under the entry with a small "t":

> a large, gallinaceous bird of the family *Meleagrididae*, esp. *Meleagris gallopava*, of America...that is domesticated in most parts of the world.[1]

(Under "gallinaceous" we find "an important-sounding word with no particular meaning.")

Turkey— definition #2

---

[1] Etymologists disagree on the derivation of the word "turkey": some assert that it comes from a confused identification of this bird with Turkish cocks and hens, while others contend that the name comes from the turkey's *turk-turk* call. By this reasoning, most people would call it a gobbly. Creative etymologists persuasively argue that "turkey" must be a corruption of the French *tour de quai* ("wharf tower") or perhaps the Italian *terra che* ("earth which").

It is the distinctive characteristics of this bird—extremely low intelligence combined with an arrogant demeanor—that have inspired Americans, ever on the lookout for a good insult, to evolve a third usage.

The most precise definition of this colloquial use of "turkey" is given by renowned turkey authority Dr. Sandra Boynton in her invaluable field guide to turkeys:[2]

A turkey is a self-righteous, intolerant, and smug incompetent.

_____

[2] *Don't Let the Turkeys Get You Down*, New York: Workman Publishing, 1986, page 11.

As the definition suggests, it is not easy to identify a turkey simply by sight. Turkeys come in many shapes, sizes, and outfits. *Behavior* is a much more reliable indicator of turkitude. But if you do happen to spot a turkey without dressing, this is basically what it looks like:

Meleagris Humanis

Side view   Front view   Doing the turkey trot

You will note that the male turkey is distinguished by a red wattle and a fanlike tail. If it seems to you that there are a disproportionate number of males depicted throughout this guide, you're probably imagining it.

IMPORTANT NOTE: The Common Turkey is often confused with the Common Nerd, perhaps because of their comparable low levels of social skills, competence, and taste. The behavior of the Turkey is often seemingly identical to the behavior of the Nerd, but there is one crucial difference: attitude. Nerds have no confidence and an excessive desire to please, whereas turkeys are exactly the reverse. For further information, please consult *A Nerdwatcher's Guide.*

The Common Nerd

Like their gallinaceous counterparts, human turkeys have been domesticated in most parts of the world. It's only a matter of time until the American terminology catches on abroad.

YOUR BASIC TURKEY

NAME:	Joe Average Citizen
RESIDES:	Anytown, U.S.A.
LATEST ACCOMPLISHMENT:	Drank a beer
QUOTE:	*"Hey, Hon, bring me another beer, willya?"*
PROFILE:	See picture above

PART ONE

TURKEYS IN GENERAL

THE WORLDWIDE TURKEY POPULATION

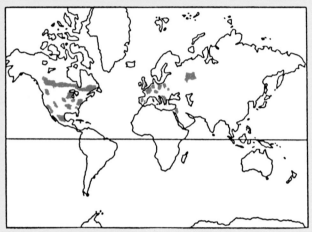

Fig. 1 Distribution of Feathered Turkeys

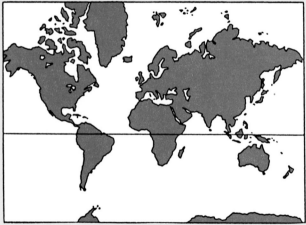

Fig. 2 Distribution of Human Turkeys

This section will provide you with useful general information about turkeys: where they come from, how they live, and how they behave.

Once you are familiar with their basic features and characteristics, turkeys are not difficult to spot. In fact, they're harder *not* to notice.

A BRIEF HISTORY

T he earliest known turkey is *Meleagranthropis,* followed by *Cro-Turgnon* and then *Neopithetic* Turkey.

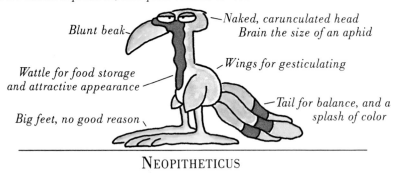

Note vacant expression, still quite evident in modern descendants

Blunt beak

Naked, carunculated head
Brain the size of an aphid

Wattle for food storage
and attractive appearance

Wings for gesticulating

Big feet, no good reason

Tail for balance, and a
splash of color

NEOPITHETICUS

A while later came the Ancient Turkeys, the most famous of which are chronicled in Pluturch.

VĒNĪ, VĪDĪ, MAENĪ, MŌ,
CACHA TĪGREM BAEDAS TŌ,
IFFĪ HOLLERS, LEDEM GŌ,
VĒNĪ, VĪDĪ, MAENĪ, MŌ.

Then there were the Dark Ages,

the Middle Ages,

the Renaissance (when just about any turkey could do anything),

and the Enlightenment.

Then came the Industrial Revolution, leading the way to mass production. Thus, by the early part of this century, the work of any one turkey could affect the lives of thousands.

And now, through the advances of modern technology, we have almost instantaneous access to important, highly specialized information.

The most significant change brought about by the Technological Revolution is in Communications. A century ago, you would only have known your local turkeys.

Today, you come into contact with more turkeys in a single week than you would once have met in an entire lifetime.

THE MATING BEHAVIOR OF TURKEYS

The most remarkable thing about any turkey is its self-confidence: absolutely unshakable, and absolutely unwarranted. Perhaps nowhere is this more remarkable than in the male of the species when his fancy turns to thoughts of love.

This sublime oblivion well protects the wooing turkey. Often he is very familiar with the dating game, but simply never realizes he is not on the team.

And sometimes, despite careful coaching, he misunderstands the game entirely.

But most turkeys eventually find someone of compatible interests and similar emotional maturity.

TURKEYS AND THEIR YOUNG

I f turkeys are good for anything, it's self-perpetuation. What turkeys lack in productivity, they more than make up for in reproductivity.

It seems unnecessary to go into the details of birthing here, since any turkey will tell you everything about her delivery at the drop of a hat.

MONDAY, APRIL 23, 3:06 A.M. : I was
abruptly awakened out of a restless sleep
by a contraction, not strong, yet different
somehow than anything I'd felt before.
"Tom!" I cried. "Wake up, Tom! I think
this is it!" Drowsily, Tom fumbled his way...

The turkey approach to child-rearing is also readily apparent, since much of it takes place in public.

Turkey parents are as rigorous about their children's education as about their behavior.

But for all their strictness, turkey parents are also extraordinarily perceptive about their children, able to see talent and intelligence that are all but invisible to anyone else.

Once you have spent time around turkey families, it is easy to start feeling superior. But before you get too smug, one word of caution: never underestimate the power and mystery of genetics.

TURKEY HABITATS

Turkeys live almost everywhere. The most obvious distinguishing feature of a turkey dwelling is that it is aggressively incongruous with its setting. In the city, you might find turkeys living here

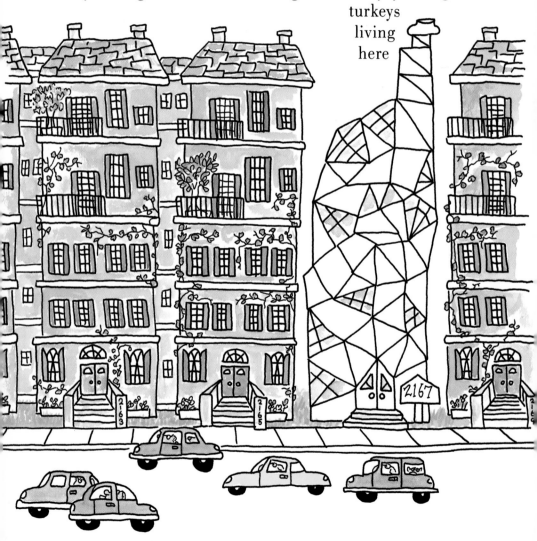

and in the country, they most likely live
in a place
like this.

Turkeys are rarely at home in the wild. When they do venture out, most often they bring their habitat with them.

The greatest concentration of turkeys is in affluent suburban areas. Spotting a turkey settlement is simple, since turkeys insist on high visibility: the residences are large and imposing, and they outnumber the trees two-to-one.

THE SOCIAL BEHAVIOR OF TURKEYS

The tendency of turkeys to flock together has had a significant impact on society at large. Because of the extraordinary size and credulity of the turkey population, any little idea that one turkey takes a liking to soon becomes a mass movement.

In fact, any trend or fashion you can name owes much of its popularity to turkeys. This would apply to anything from clothes and speech—

to recreation—

all the way to philosophical movements.

Turkeys accept any new fashion with great energy, and as easily reject old passions.

Once started, a movement will gain many turkey followers simply by virtue of its popularity. Being "current" lends an air of authority to any turkey.

Because of their enthusiasm and sheer numbers, turkeys are the single most powerful political force in this or any country—but a very fickle force, too.

Swing to the left! Swing to the right! Stand up, sit down, FIGHT, FIGHT, FIGHT!

Above all, turkeys thrive in any movement that emphasizes self (with the obvious exception of self-basting).

In the 60s, it was Finding Yourself and Helping Others.

In the 70s, it was Loving Yourself and Accepting Others.

And now in the 80s, it's Indulging Yourself and What Others?

... Why settle for just a PIECE of the pie
when you can HAVE THE WHOLE PIE?
If someone else wants some, tell him to
get his own pie! Why feel guilty?
You didn't make the world.
   You deserve whatever you want,
     because YOU'RE WORTH IT —
just by being part of this exciting
new generation of
Young Urbane Poultry!

SENSE OF HUMOR

The sense of humor of a turkey is distinguished by four basic features:

First, it is insensitive.

Second, it is predictable.

Third, it is unwise.

And last, it is nonreciprocal.

A GUIDE TO TURKEY CALLS

YOUNG: A whining, high-pitched
Nahidonwannadodat, Iwannadodis

SOCIAL: *Blatherblatherblatherblather*
spoken continuously at high volume

COURTING: ♂ A wolfish whistle, followed by a jaunty
and low-pitched *Hey hey hey! Hey hey hey!*

♀ A heavily inflected and high-pitched
whyhel-LO! Tee-hee, tee-hee, tee-hee

WARNING: A full-voiced *HEDZUP! HEDZUP!*
HEYOOALL, HEDZUP!

PANIC: A squealing squawk *i-wan-mi-MA-mee!*

FLOCK CALL: *kMON, GUYS, lezGO lezGO!* Answered by
Heerwecum! Heerwecum!

STANDARD TURKEY UNCONSCIOUSNESS FACTOR TEST (S.T.U.F.T.)

Have you ever begun a sentence with "Frankly"?

Have you ever ended a sentence with "if you catch my drift"?

Do you own time in a time-share condominium?

Do you routinely buy flight insurance?

Do you wax your car at least once a week?

When dressing, do you always put on your socks first?

Do you have a collection of any sort?

Do you smoke?

Do you live in a Colonial house built in the last thirty years?

Do you know more than three Knock-knock jokes?

Do you have any records by The Lettermen?

Can you defend polyester?

Would you like to go to Disney World?

Do you find tests like this a challenge?

Would you continue answering questions all the way to the end?

Including this one?

How about this?

HOW TO SCORE: If you answered anything other than "NO" to more than one question, it is important that you buy 12 more copies of this book. Trust me.

YES	NO	MAYBE	COULD YOU REPEAT THE QUESTION?	I DON'T HAVE TO ANSWER THAT!
☐	☐	☐	☐	☐
☐	☐	☐	☐	☐
☐	☐	☐	☐	☐
☐	☐	☐	☐	☐
☐	☐	☐	☐	☐
☐	☐	☐	☐	☐
☐	☐	☐	☐	☐
☐	☐	☐	☐	☐
☐	☐	☐	☐	☐
☐	☐	☐	☐	☐
☐	☐	☐	☐	☐
☐	☐	☐	☐	☐
☐	☐	☐	☐	☐
☐	☐	☐	☐	☐
☐	☐	☐	☐	☐
☐	☐	☐	☐	☐
☐	☐	☐	☐	☐
TOTAL				

A CONTEMPORARY ARTIST

NAME: Chrisco

RESIDES: New York City

LATEST ACCOMPLISHMENT: Just completed plans to cover the entire city of Chicago—buildings, cars, buses, trees, grass, pigeons— with vermilion paint. (Proposal is temporarily stalled in nonvisionary City Council.) To be entitled *Painting the Town Red.*

QUOTE: *"The world is a huge canvas, and the canvas is a huge world. Only God can make a tree, but only Man would dream of wrapping it in aluminum foil."*

PROFILE: Bold. Daring. Adventurous. A Little Flaky.

PART TWO

THE PROFESSIONAL TURKEY

THE BUREAUCRATIC TURKEY

I n Part Two, you will be introduced to Professional Turkeys—although I suspect you've met before.

Because of limitations of space and good will, not all callings are included here. I have chosen to survey those professions in which there is the greatest density of turkeys. The selection wasn't easy, given that turkeys in any profession are nothing if not dense.

Nope. Don't see anything right off that can explain that growling and thudding noise you describe.

THE TURKEY PHYSICIAN

There is widespread opinion that all doctors are turkeys. This is simply not true. There are seventeen exceptions in the United States alone.

The most distinctive characteristic of a Medical Turkey is its very large bill. The bill increases in size for every year the doctor has spent in professional training, so the bill of a surgeon is particularly stunning.

Turkey doctors have a policy of keeping their waiting rooms full at all times. This is achieved by scheduling patients at ten-minute intervals,* and seeing them at seventy-minute intervals.

Patients (sic) is a virtue.

---

*If you have a 3:20 appointment and it turns out that the guy next to you also has a 3:20 appointment, you might suspect that the doctor schedules patients for the *exact same time;* actually, the other guy's been waiting since 3:20 yesterday.

Doctors use this full-waiting-room policy not only to enhance their own image of being in great demand, but also to give their patients the opportunity to become friendly with people and germs that they otherwise might never have met.

After a patient has spent the prerequisite hours in the waiting room, he can anticipate some stern words from the doctor.

Turkey doctors are always emphatic, if not always correct, about what is best for a patient's well-being.

Many Medical Turkeys deal with patients simply by speaking as clearly and succinctly as they write.

But there is one thing more unsettling than a doctor who lacks a bedside manner, and that is the turkey who has taken pains (heh heh) to acquire one.

Beauty Salons (cont'd)

FOLLICLE FROLICLE
170 Main . . . . .TU 9-0417

HAIR IT IS
Pleasant Blvd . . . . . .TU 7-6767

HAIR TODAY, GONE TOMORROW
63 Ellett. 879-6411

HAIRITAGE
1852 Albany Tnpk . . .482-2162

HAIRPORT
21 Colebrook Rd . . .TU 9-3118
(SEE ADVERTISEMENT THIS PAGE)

HEADQUARTERS BEAUTY SALON
283 Carolina . . . . . .TU 7-6431

HEADSHOPPE
Miles St. 835-0066

HEAVEN

MONSIEUR DINDON
Main La 482-1122
(SEE ADVERTISEMENT THIS PAGE)

PERMANENT FIXTURE
2380 Mountain Av . . .879-4158
(SEE ADVERTISEMENT THIS PAGE)

SHEAR DELIGHT
118 Elm. . . . . .TU 7-2628

SHEAR EMBARRASSMENT
Mt. Avon . . . . .TU 9-1656

TRESS FOR SUCCESS
60 Main. 835-1113

WAVE GOODBYE
Kings Plaza,
114 Main . . . . .TU 7-0853
(SEE ADVERTISEMENT THIS PAGE)

WHOOPING COIFF
53 Center St 835-0920

Beer & Ale—Retail
See "Liquors Retail"

Bells & Chimes
See "Chimes & Bells"

THE TURKEY HAIRSTYLIST

You can almost always tell a turkey beautician by the name of the shop. Though any turkey will gobble up a pun, hairdressers seem to think of *part*-icularly many, most of them quite hyst-*hair*-ical. (SEE ADVERTISEMENTS OPPOSITE PAGE)

Even if you take care to choose a salon with a dignified name—

—there may yet be a turkey lurking within, ready to turn your ho-hum hairstyle into a dramatic creation.

THE INSURANCE TURKEY

The turkey in insurance is trained to be a stabilizing influence on clients. When you are content, your agent reminds you of the undercurrent of catastrophe in all our lives.

Supposing, God Forbid, that anything should happen to your car or, God Forbid, your house or even to you, God Forbid?

Supposing a terrible tornado hit just two days after you had fractured your wrist in a brutal skiing accident, and while you were trying to clear away some of the considerable debris — using your one good arm as best you could — a gang of rotten thieves came marauding in and stole your last remaining items of value?

Well, we want to be there. We want to take your troubles and make them ours, God Forbid.

And when you are distraught, your agent is a model of serenity.

Mel Gallopavo here ... Oh, really? Gee,
that's too bad. Anything of value taken? ...
Oh, really? Gosh, what a shame.
   Well, all you need to do is to send us a
photograph of the burglar and ... You didn't?
Hmm... I'm afraid that makes things more
complicated. All right, for now just send us
 snapshots of all the stolen items and ···
You don't? Hmmmm... Okay, I tell you what:
 just have all your bills of sale notarized
and send ... what?... Well, where are they, then?
 ... It seems to me you're trying to make it
as difficult as possible for us to consider
    your claim...

SERVICE AND REPAIR TURKEYS

Perhaps the most ubiquitous of all is the Service and Repair Turkey. You may be wondering why anyone would trust a turkey to do repairs in the first place. The reason is simply that it's usually not obvious that a repairman is a turkey until it's too late.

Golly! Look at all these wires and things.

If you do suspect that the worker who shows up at your house is a turkey, make sure that you give him very specific instructions about what you want done. Never leave anything to his professional judgment.

Yeah, well you didn't say NOT to put all the switches in the same location, either!

Of course, even a homeowner who has given the most meticulous directions is still not assured of her intended results.

And sometimes a repair turkey has such a Take Charge attitude, the homeowner may be reluctant to offer any advice at all.

THE TURKEY ARCHITECT

Any turkey architect worth his gravy considers himself an artist first, a professional second. Or last. Many architects are such purists that they spend three rigorous years in architecture school working on handwriting alone.

Then, once the difficult penmanship has been mastered, the architurk-in-training goes on to a three-year apprenticeship in a large firm, practicing and perfecting his drafting technique and model-construction skills.

A typical turkey apprentice works a sixty-five-hour week, eschewing the frivolities of television, parties, games, and structural engineering. At the end of this single-minded six years of training, there is a difficult certification examination that includes such questions as *"What architect designed the Guggenheim Museum?"*

    ☐ Palladio   ☐ Orville Wright
    ☐ Frank Lloyd Wright ☐ You

(But not so challenging as to include *"Which way does water flow?* ☐ Uphill ☐ Downhill ☐ Laterally ☐ North.")

Once certified, the turkey architect is ready to open his own office. When you commission him to design a building, you are assured of getting plans that are beautiful enough to hang on your wall.

Whether or not you get a wall structurally sound enough to hang the plans on is somewhat more iffy.

THE TURKEY AS PSYCHOLOGIST

Turkeys abound in the Social Sciences in general, and in Psychology in particular. Turkey psychologists conduct painstaking and exhaustive experiments, in order to prove conclusively those things that we could previously only guess at with 97% accuracy.

These are among their most significant findings to date:

1. If you starve a rat for three days, then offer it the choice of food or listening to Beethoven, most rats will choose food. (This finding has led to significant speculation on the importance of aesthetic experience vis-à-vis survival.)

2. Subjects who live in small, dark rooms working twelve hours a day for four years tend to be more cynical and depressed than those living lives of leisure in spacious homes for the same length of time. (Conclusion based on observation of graduate students in Psychology in Group A, faculty and administration in Group B.)

3. Misery has a love/hate relationship with company.

THE TURKEY PSYCHIATRIST

TURKEYS IN TEACHING

All turkey educators know that for every level of teaching, there is only one correct approach.

In Early Education, a teacher must be supportive and patient—

—although still careful not to lose sight of Standards.

As students grow, they become ready for more structured guidance.

All right, Class, now I'm going to read you two letters, and I want you to listen carefully:

Dear Mary,
I want you to know how much I enjoyed our weekend at the shore. It was a nice change of pace for me, and it was great fun being with you and your family.

Thanks a million,
Carol

Now here's the second letter:

Dear Mary,
The billowy waves crashing upon the shore, the plaintive cries of the circling gulls far above our heads, the whoosh and whirr of the sand stirred by angry winds: all these impressions yet linger. Thank you for these cherished memories.

With gratitude,
Carol

Now: who can tell me which is the more effective letter, because of its vivid word choice and attention to detail?

By the time students reach college, they can no longer expect to be so gently nurtured. Professorial turkeys are rigorous and unyielding in their demand for excellence from their students.

THE TURKEY AS SALES CLERK

ON THE CAMPAIGN TRAIL

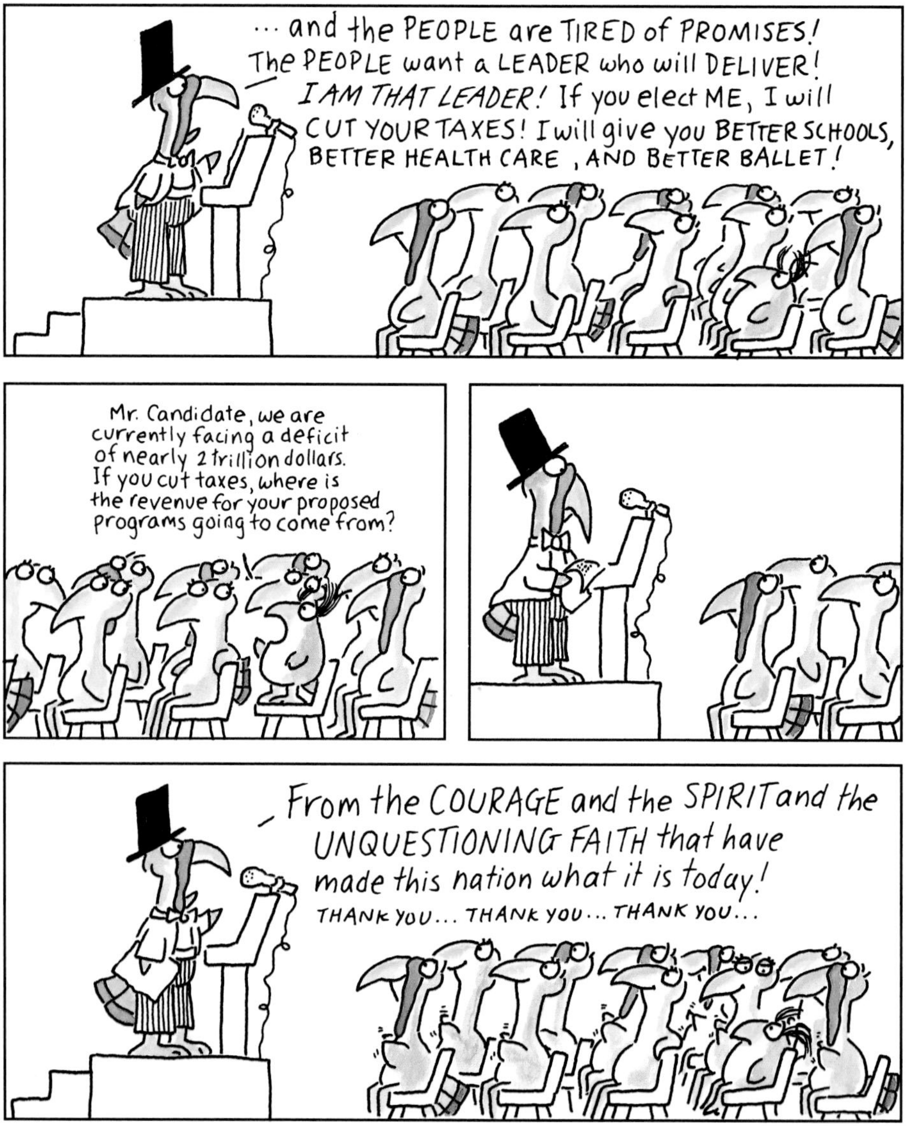
... and the PEOPLE are TIRED of PROMISES! The PEOPLE want a LEADER who will DELIVER! I AM THAT LEADER! If you elect ME, I will CUT YOUR TAXES! I will give you BETTER SCHOOLS, BETTER HEALTH CARE, AND BETTER BALLET!
Mr. Candidate, we are currently facing a deficit of nearly 2 trillion dollars. If you cut taxes, where is the revenue for your proposed programs going to come from?
From the COURAGE and the SPIRIT and the UNQUESTIONING FAITH that have made this nation what it is today!
THANK YOU... THANK YOU... THANK YOU...

TURKEYS IN GOVERNMENT

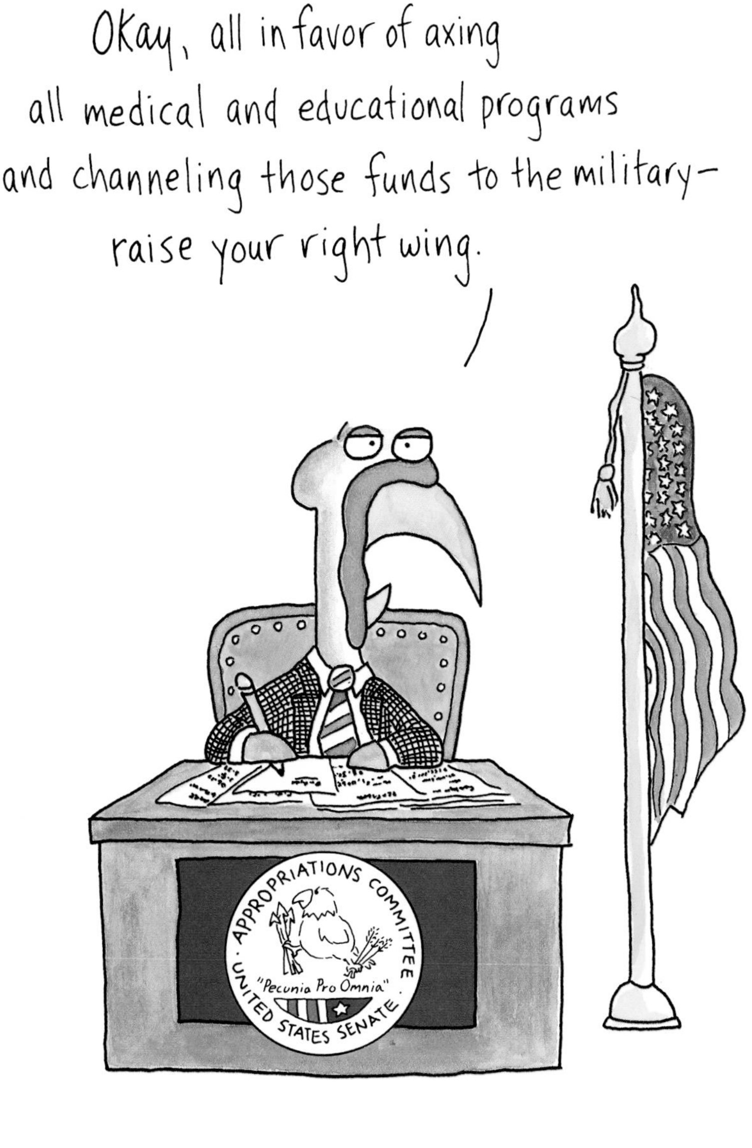
Okay, all in favor of axing all medical and educational programs and channeling those funds to the military— raise your right wing.
APPROPRIATIONS COMMITTEE
"Pecunia Pro Omnia"
UNITED STATES SENATE

THE TURKEY IN REAL ESTATE

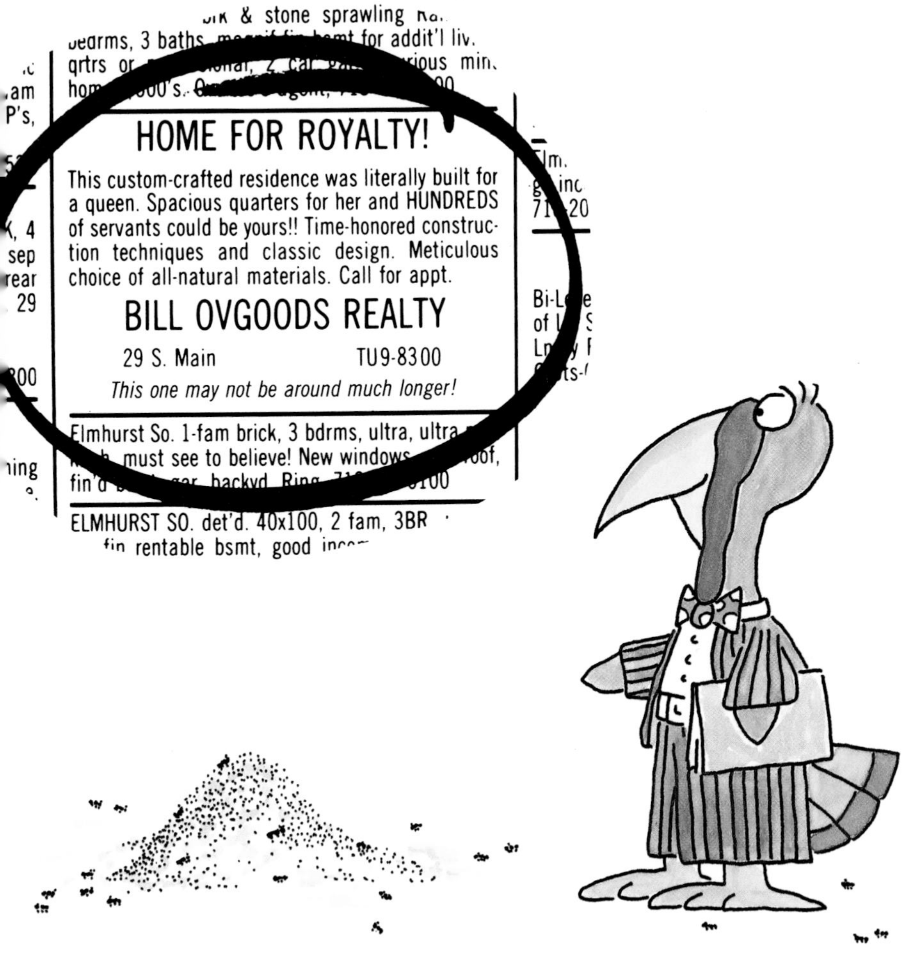
HOME FOR ROYALTY!
This custom-crafted residence was literally built for a queen. Spacious quarters for her and HUNDREDS of servants could be yours!! Time-honored construction techniques and classic design. Meticulous choice of all-natural materials. Call for appt.
BILL OVGOODS REALTY
29 S. Main TU9-8300
This one may not be around much longer!
ELMHURST SO. det'd. 40x100, 2 fam, 3BR

TURKEYS IN BUSINESS

The turkey in business is often very adept at identifying problems in the company.

And a turkey can always find the perfect solution.

VARIOUS SUCCESSFUL PRODUCTS INTRODUCED BY TURKEYS OVER THE PAST 75 YEARS

DIGITAL CLOCKS
ELECTRIC BUG-ZAPPERS
TRASH COMPACTORS
WOOD-GRAIN-LOOK PLASTIC
NON-DAIRY CREAMER
TINSEL
CAROB
GREETING CARDS
ROOM DEODORIZERS
SALAD SPINNERS
FUZZY TOILET TANK COVERS
HERBAL TEA
TANNING SALONS
DIRT BIKES
ALCOHOL-REMOVED WINE
PLASTIC GRASS
MACRAMÉ
FLUORESCENT LIGHTS
MARGARINE
MUZAK
DESTRUCTOBOT™ CALCULATORS*
MISS WONDERLOVELY™ CALCULATORS*

*To be introduced next August, but included here because of extraordinary advance sales of $6.6 billion.

THE ATTURKEY-AT-LAW

Why do you need a lawyer at all? That's a very good question. Let me see if I can clarify that for you.

In the event that the party of the first part (hereinafter sometimes referred to as "you") were to handle your affairs *in pro per* without benefit of a duly engaged legal counsel, you would be subject to numerous difficulties, obstacles, and obstructions.

To wit: the party of the first part so unencumbered of said counsel of a legal nature would be unequipped to manufacture, endure, and/or disentangle the concomitant accumulation of ad hoc legal appropriation of the language.

If you do decide to engage my services, I will consider this a courtesy consultation. If not, cough up seventy smackers.

THE EDITOR TURKEY

As should be obvious to anyone, the phrase "editor turkey" is a contradiction in terms, for editors are the unsung heroes and heroines of book publishing. Thank you.

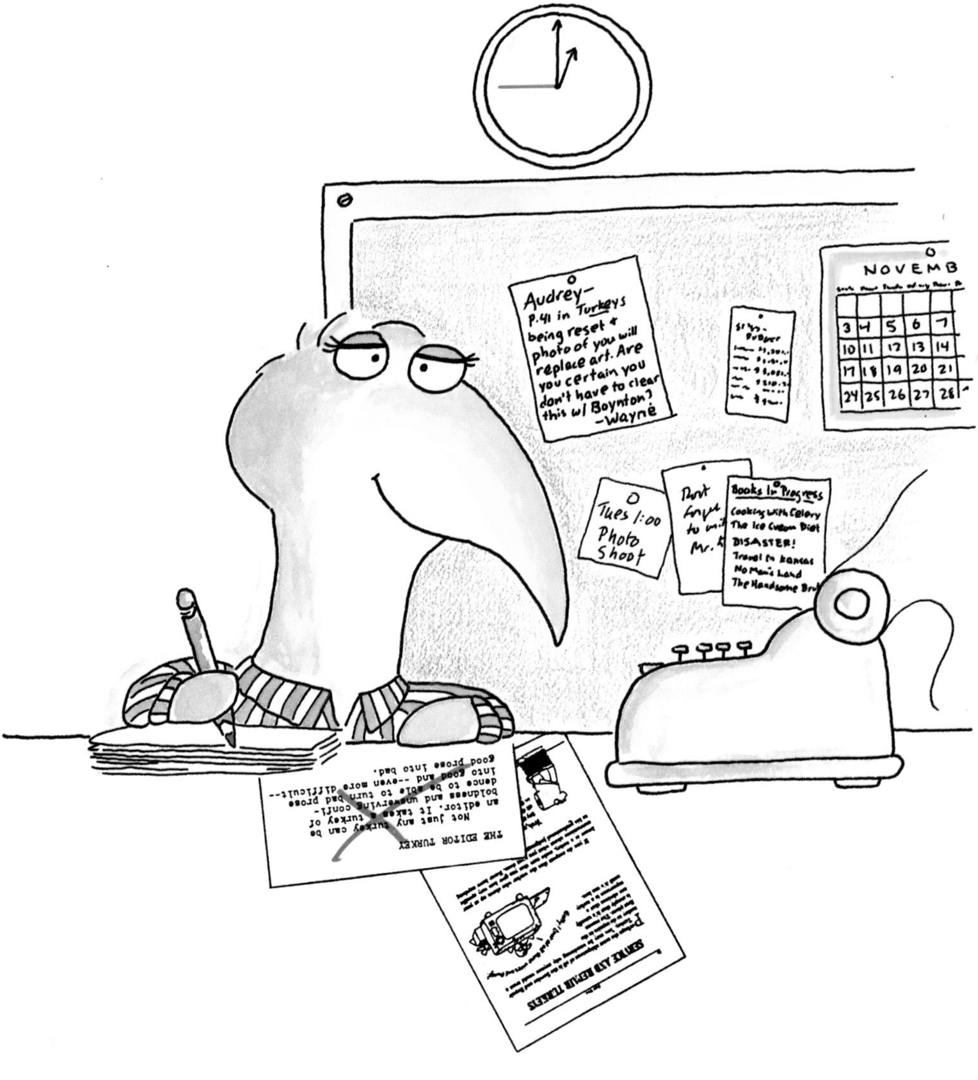
Audrey—
P.41 in Turkeys being reset & photo of you will replace art. Are you certain you don't have to clear this w/ Boynton?
—Wayne
NOVEMB
Tues 1:00 Photo Shoot
Books In Progress
Cooking with Celery
The Ice Cream Diet
DISASTER!
Travel in Kansas
No Man's Land

TURKEY OF THE SLOPES

NAME:	Marie Claude Jambe-Cassée
RESIDES:	Kansas
LATEST ACCOMPLISHMENT:	First skier ever to descend Breakneck Run entirely on hands and knees.
QUOTE:	*"Aieeeeee!"*
PROFILE:	Hat matches sweater, which matches knickers, which match socks, which match boots. In fact, everything is well coordinated, except Marie Claude.

PART THREE

TURKEYS AT LEISURE

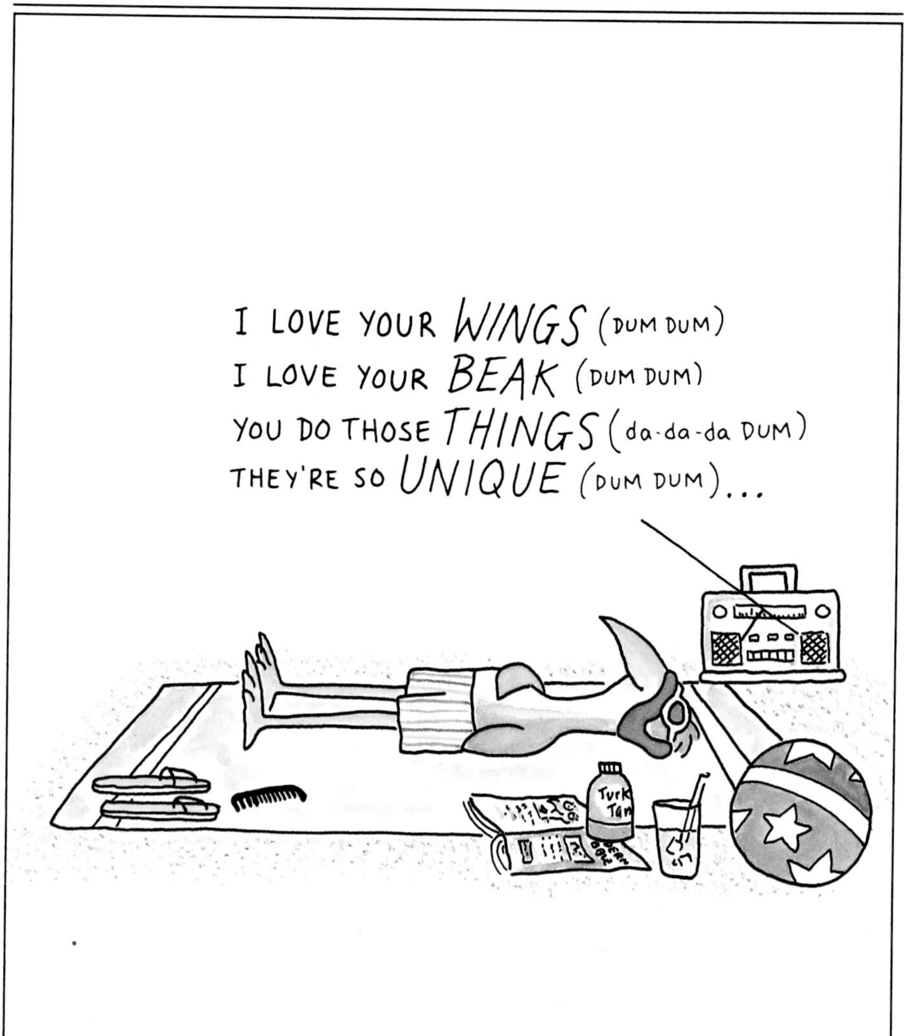
I LOVE YOUR WINGS (DUM DUM)
I LOVE YOUR BEAK (DUM DUM)
YOU DO THOSE THINGS (da-da-da DUM)
THEY'RE SO UNIQUE (DUM DUM)...
Turk Tan

In this last section, we will take a look at turkeys at play: their favorite pastimes and amusements, including sports, entertainment, and social life.

You will discover here that turkeys can really enjoy themselves—which is a good thing since no one else really enjoys them.

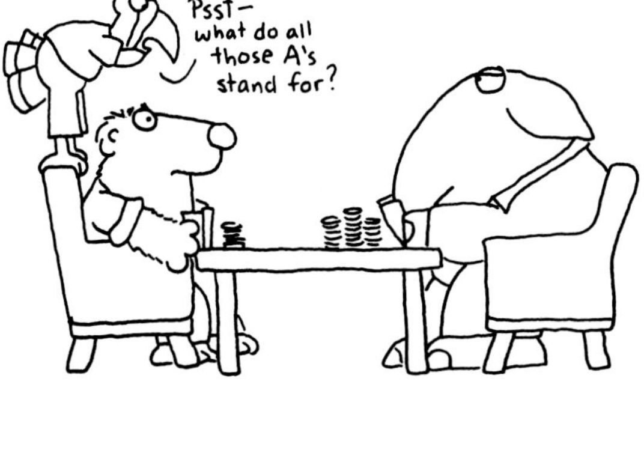
Psst–
what do all
those A's
stand for?

A TURKEY'S IDEA OF A GOOD TIME

Turkeys love to feel superior to everyone else. And many turkeys know that being braver, kinder, more athletic, more skilled, stronger, and smarter have nothing to do with being better. Being *faster* is all that counts—hence the popularity among turkeys of motorized vehicles.

Speed turkeys' real thrills come not so much from speed as from the harassment of anyone who is self-propelling, whether in cycling,

boating,

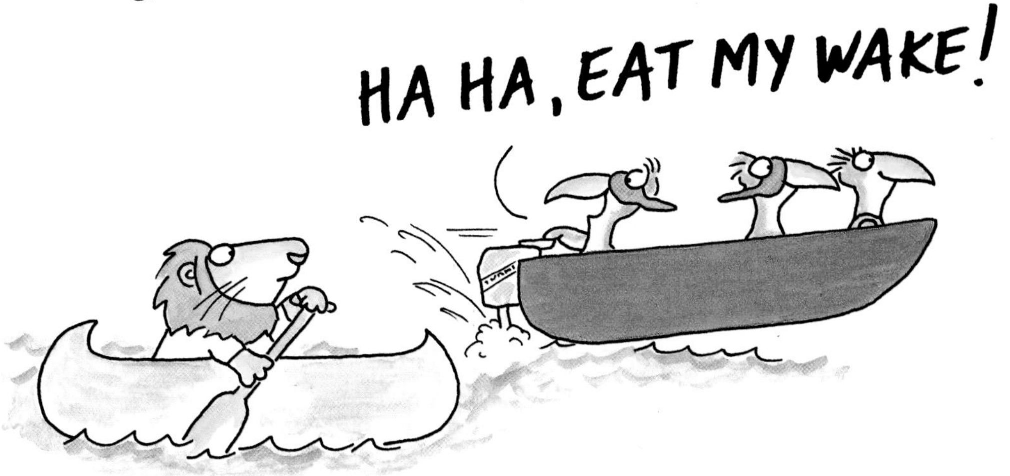
HA HA, EAT MY WAKE!

or skiing.

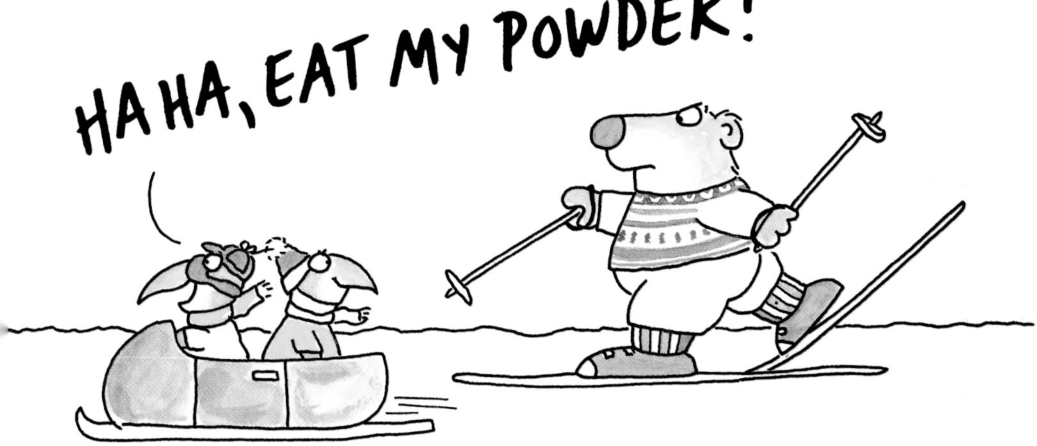
HA HA, EAT MY POWDER!

Occasionally it does happen that a turkey's sense of superiority is temporarily shaken, when he misjudges his advantage.

TURKEY FITNESS

Ambitious turkeys shun fast forward mobility in favor of rapid upward mobility. Today's image-conscious turkey knows that How You Look is what really matters. If you look good, you feel good; and if you feel good, you impress good. That's why so many turkeys have made an investment in running—

—because running clothes make you look good, without all the discomfort and inconvenience of exercise.

But there are turkey runners who believe that it's not enough just to spend a lot of money on the right outfit. To get real mileage, you have to acquire the vocabulary, too.

... but, boy, you don't know what RUNNER's HIGH is until you've had that SECOND WIND kick in after HITTING THE WALL on kilometer 7 of a 10-k race!

A few hard-core turkey running enthusiasts resort to actual running, and therefore move on to a more advanced vocabulary, including things like "pronation," "shin splints," "orthotics," and "acute bilateral tendinitis."

Many other upscale turkeys seek the cachet that comes with pursuing a sport that is more exclusive than running, but that still has attractive clothes. These turkeys join a Country Club (so named because "Suburbs Club," though more accurate, doesn't have the same ring) and play tennis.

For those who want the prestige of membership yet prefer clothes that actually *undermine* their appearance, Country Clubs also offer golf.

City dwellers usually join Health Clubs, which offer them all the visibility and expense of Country Clubs, plus invaluable instruction.

The most gutsy turkeys shun the comfort and easy prestige of close-to-home exercise, choosing to affect instead an image of rugged outdoorsiness. These turkeys enter the dangerous and uncertain world of whitewater canoeing—

or rock-climbing—

or mail-ordering.

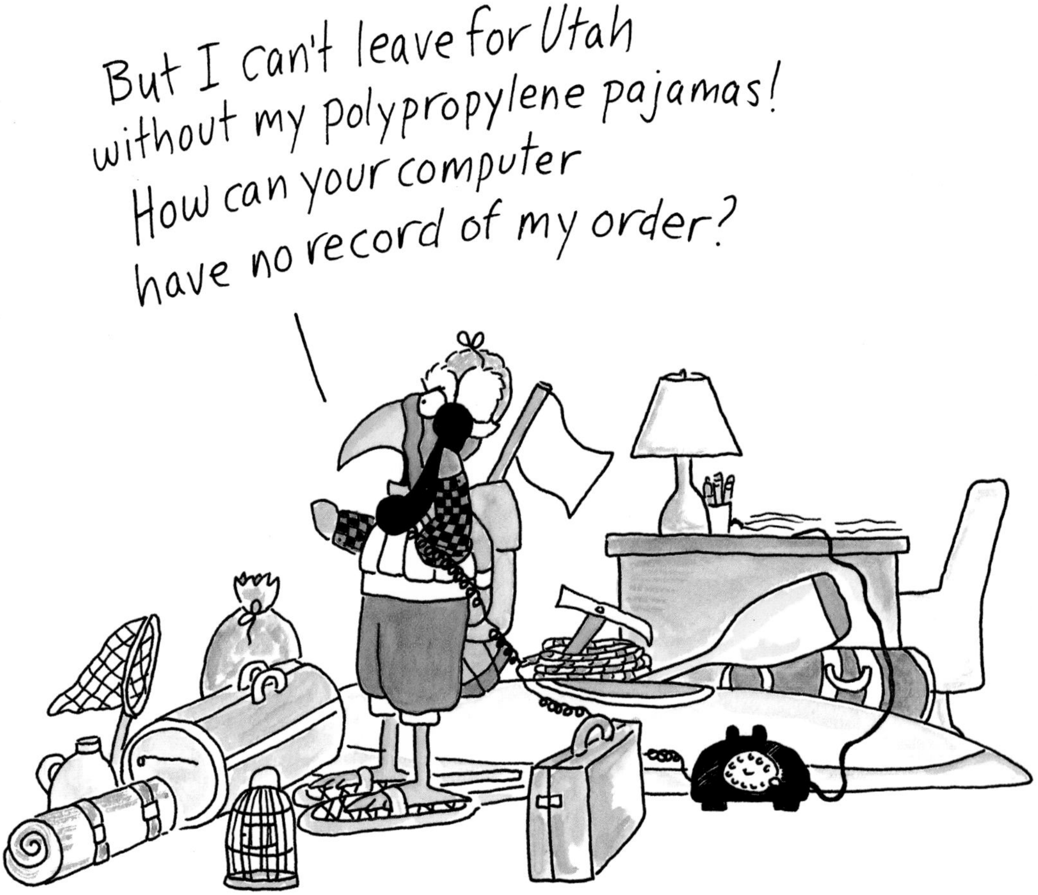
But I can't leave for Utah without my polypropylene pajamas! How can your computer have no record of my order?

VISITING TURKEYS

"If you're ever in the neighborhood, stop by and see us."
Most everyone knows that this polite social convention simply means "I can't think of anything more to say to you." But what is obvious to any half-intelligent human being is not necessarily obvious to any turkey.

... and just outside Ann Arbor
we said to ourselves, "You know,
the Bassetts aren't too far from
here. Why don't we just swing by
New Hampshire and spend
July at their place?"

Once you realize what turkeys will construe as an invitation, you should be able to avoid ever doing it again. If you're paying attention.

Even if you manage to avoid turkeys as company, you may have to consent to having them be your hosts.

You might be worried about what you'll find to talk about all evening. But conversation before dinner is not a problem: while your hosts prepare the meal, you will be seated in the living room so you can just relax.

And conversation during dinner is no problem, since your turkey hosts will spend the whole time reciting what went into this evening's meal.

And conversation after dinner is no problem: the evening is over exactly two minutes before *Family Feud* comes on.

AT A PARTY

The turkeys are the ones who arrive early and stay through breakfast. For the most part they try to dominate the party, although there is always one who sits off to the side, complaining to anyone who tries to draw her into the group.

It's all so shallow and meaningless. Don't they realize how rotten things are out there? Doesn't anybody care? I mean, why even HAVE parties, anyway?

There is usually at least one turkey who considers himself the life of the party,

and another who tries to be the soul of wit.

Sooner or later, some turkey is bound to organize a party game—most likely Charades.

As the party wears on, whole groups of turkeys will take to singing old favorites.

There is even some evidence that suggests that anyone who goes to parties at all is a turkey. Don't give it a second thought.

TURKEYS ON THE TOWN

With the advent of video cassette recorders, more and more turkeys are able now to go out in the evening.

... and remember to push
"SIMUL REC" and "6"
when you turn
"Dallas" on. In case
of an emergency, here's
a list of VCR repair
numbers. And
be sure to
call us immediately
if J.R. is arrested
or indicted.

Restaurants have benefited most from this surge of turkeys into nighttime society. Once, a restaurant became successful simply by serving food that tasted good. Now, thanks to the demands of discerning turkey diners, today's *restaurateurs* are emphasizing *novelty of presentation,* and their efforts have elevated restaurant food to the status of Art.

... and our *soup du jour* is "Warhol Tomato."
This is a nostalgic *potage* served cold in a vivid red and white unopened can.
    For our entrées, this evening's fish is "Jackson Pollack." This is a fresh pollack filet, whimsically spattered with red, blue, yellow and black sauces...

Have you anything more Minimalist?

After sorbet and cappuccino, how do turkeys spend the rest of an evening out? Some turkeys love to go dancing.

Others find it restful to go to a thought-provoking play.

All the rest go to concerts—and their taste in music runs the gamut.

TASTE IN MUSIC SPECTRUM

AT THE MOVIES

The most popular pastime for turkeys is going to the movies. The first place you might spot one is at the box office.

If the turkey has never seen the film before, he will behave much as if he were a radio announcer at a sporting event:

If he has seen the film already, a turkey enjoys previewing memorable segments for anyone watching the movie for the first time:

And if the turkey has seen the film many times, those in the rows ahead will hear most of the dialogue in stereo ⎯⎯⎯⎯→

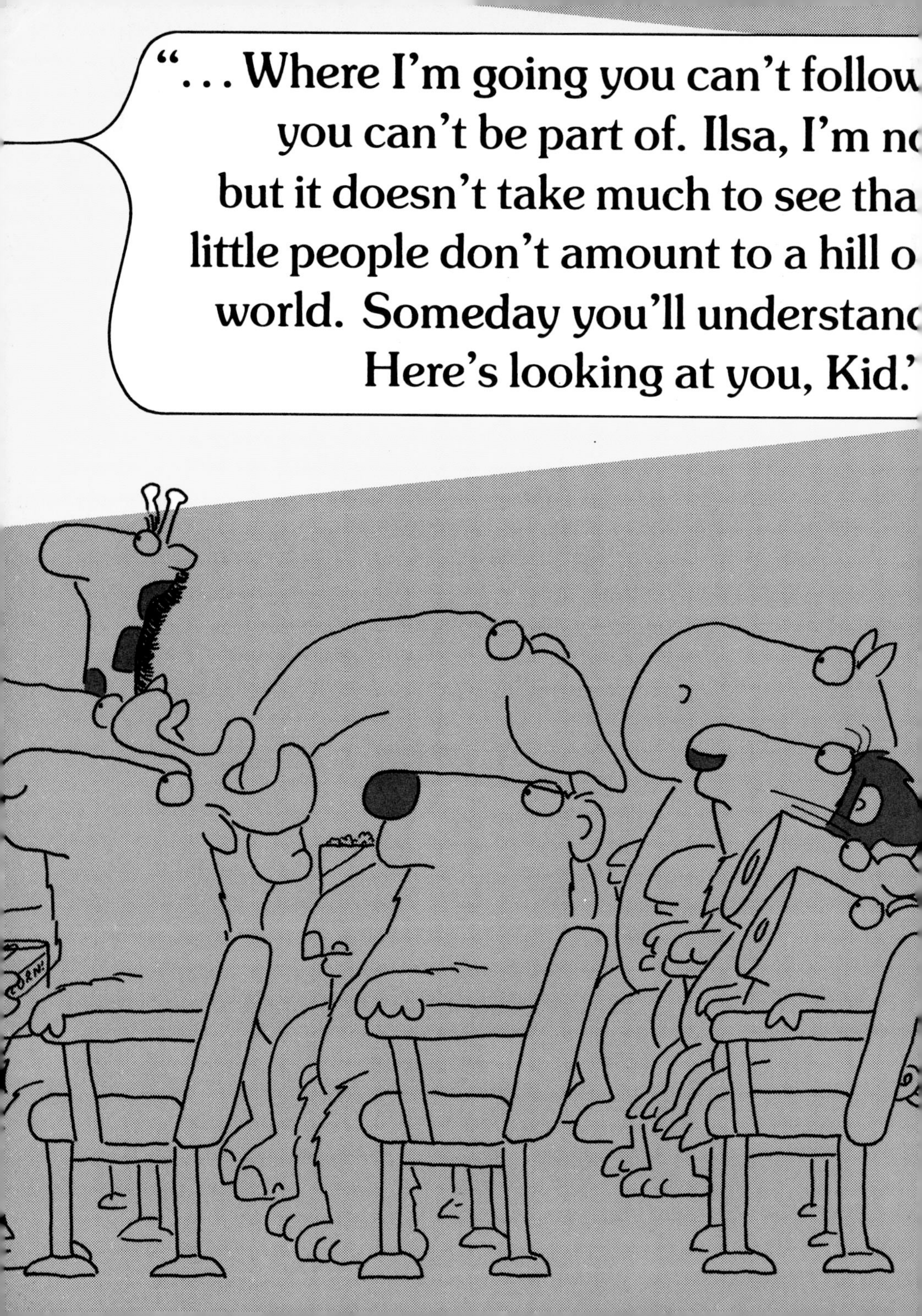
“. . . Where I’m going you can’t follo
you can’t be part of. Ilsa, I’m n
but it doesn’t take much to see tha
little people don’t amount to a hill o
world. Someday you’ll understan
Here’s looking at you, Kid.

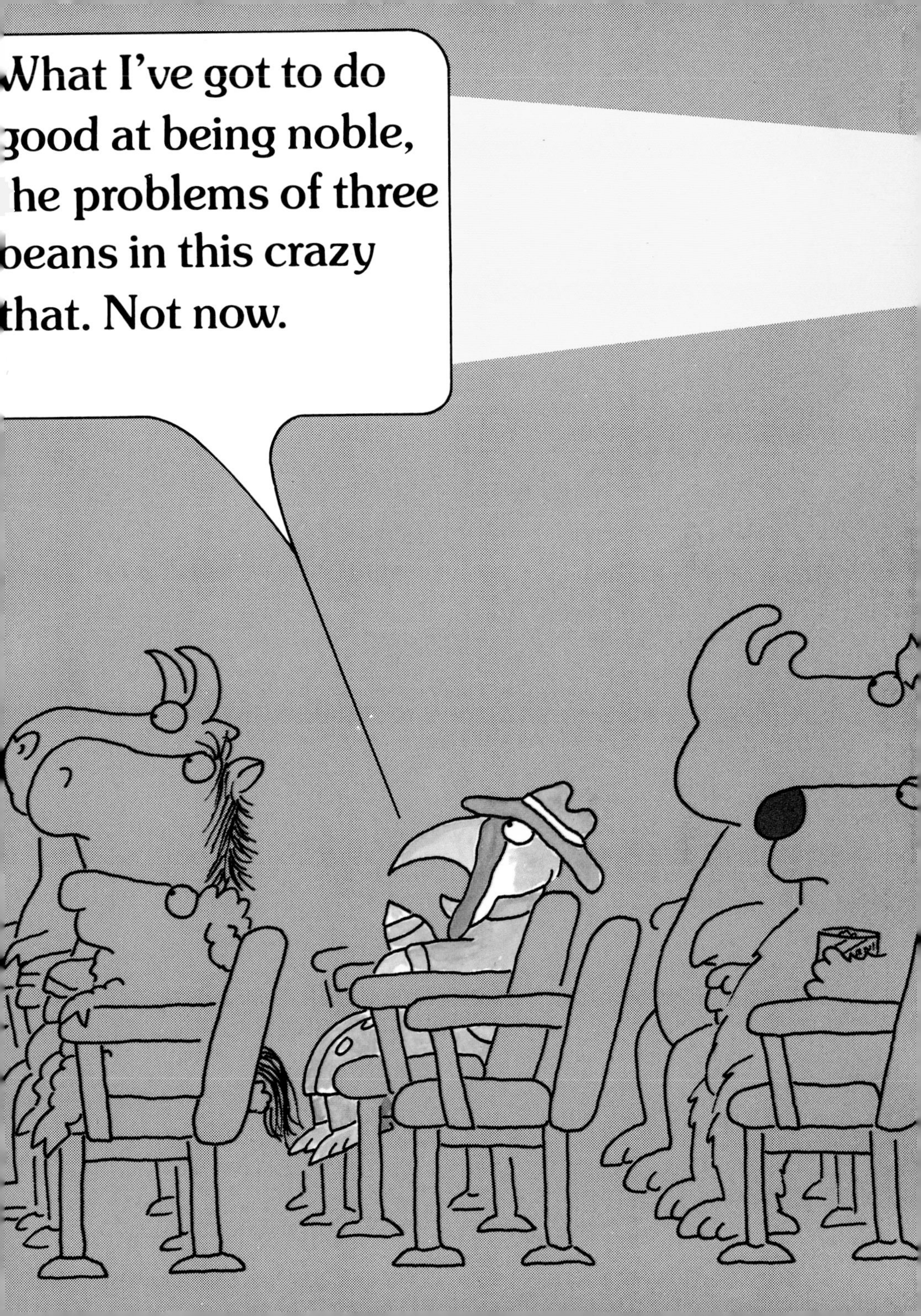
What I’ve got to do
good at being noble,
he problems of three
beans in this crazy
that. Not now.

AFTERWORD

I have tried to make this field guide comprehensive, knowing all the while that the task is simply not humanly possible. Many readers will be disappointed that their own pet turkeys have been either omitted or overlooked, and for that I am sorry.

But I hope that you have found this guide to be informative, and that you will continue to consult it whenever necessary.

There is one last thing about turkeys that has not been mentioned, yet which may be the single most important turkey fact. Nonetheless, I hesitate to bring it up for fear that it might put some beaks out of joint.

However, professional responsibility must outweigh personal reservations, so here it is:

A TURKEY SELDOM KNOWS THAT IT IS A TURKEY.

BOY, I SURE ENJOYED THAT BOOK! IT REALLY NAILED THOSE TURKEYS!

APPENDIX

NOTE: Comprehensive statistical information was supposed to have been included here, comprised of 27 pages of detailed charts, maps, graphs, and tables. However, this would have substantially increased the size and price of the volume, so professional advice prevailed.

You know, winter's coming on...

...and it occurred to me that maybe we should get some of those new insulated drapes to cut down the draft.

I hardly think that the up-front dollars and the relatively low R-value of the drapes would compare favorably with the alternative of bricking the windows up.

WHY ARE YOU STARING AT ME?

No reason... no reason...

The author would like to offer thanksgiving to:

Paul Hanson
Geoffrey Strachan
Edite Kroll
Cathy Hearn
Jamie McEwan
Suzanne Rafer
Peter & Carolan Workman
Wayne Kirn
Joanne Strauss
Ludvik Tomazic

Famous Poultry Design School

asks:

CAN YOU DRAW THIS TURKEY?

Just Some of Our Faculty
RED WATTEAU
LEONARD DA MINCEMEAT
VINCENT VAN GOBBLE

YOU may be one of the credulous artists we're looking for!
THIS may be the beginning of an exciting career in
turkigraphy,
IF YOU QUALIFY!
IMAGINE: the prestige of being a real <u>Turkey Artist!</u>

87% of our graduates go on to work!

"HOW DO I QUALIFY?" Just send us your drawing of our charming
friend (above), or print the words "CUTE TURKEY" on a 3 x 5 card.
Enclose with it a check for $500.00 (in case you qualify, we know you'll
want to start immediately!) to:

Famous Poultry Design School
c/o Workman Publishing Company, Inc.
1 West 39th Street
New York, NY 10018

CUT

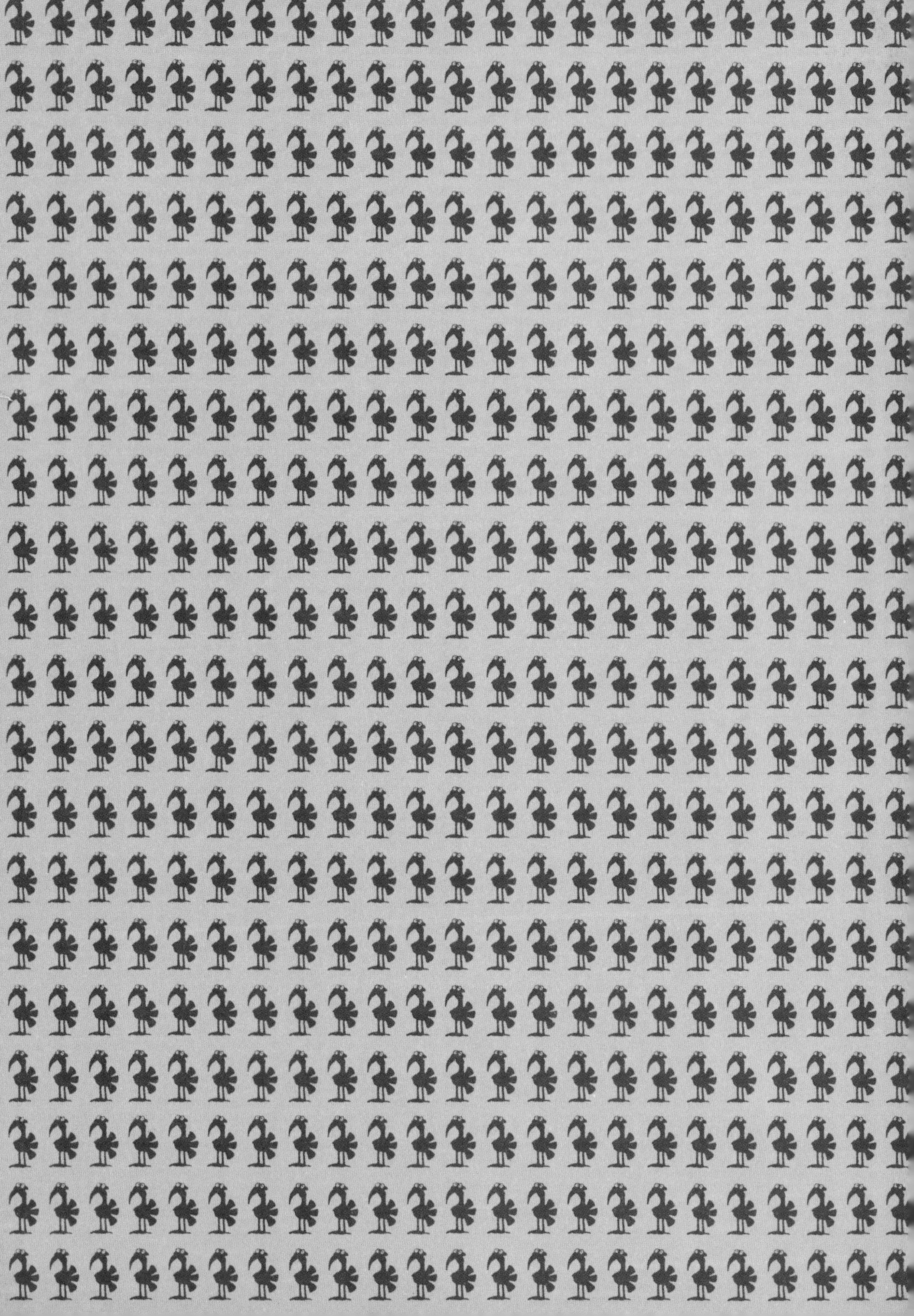